WISE QUOTES: PLATO

(150 PLATO QUOTES)

Vol. 1

Rowan Stevens

A dog has the soul of a philosopher.

A hero is born among a hundred, a wise man is found among a thousand, but an accomplished one might not be found even among a hundred thousand men.

A house that has a library in it has a soul.

A life without investigation is not worth living.

According to Diotima, Love is not a god at all, but is rather a spirit that mediates between people and the objects of their desire. Love is neither wise nor beautiful, but is rather the desire for wisdom and beauty.

All I really know is the extent of my own ignorance.

All is flux, nothing stays still.

All learning has an emotional base.

An empty vessel makes the loudest sound, so they that have the least wit are the greatest babblers.

And so, when a person meets the half that is his very own, whatever his orientation, whether it's to young men or not, then something wonderful happens: the two are struck from their senses by love, by a sense of belonging to one another, and by desire, and they don't want to be separated from one another, not even for a moment.

Any man may easily do harm, but not every man can do good to another.

Astronomy compels the soul to look upwards and leads us from this world to another.

At the touch of love everyone becomes a poet.

Be kind, because everyone is having a really hard time.

Be kind, for everyone you meet is fighting a harder battle.

Beauty lies in the eyes of the beholder.

Beauty of style and harmony and grace and good rhythm depend on simplicity.

Bodily exercise, when compulsory, does no harm to the body; but knowledge which is acquired under compulsion obtains no hold on the mind.

Books are immortal sons defying their sires.

But above all things truth beareth away the victory.

Calligraphy is a geometry of the soul which manifests itself physically.

Character is simply habit long continued.

Come then, and let us pass a leisure hour in storytelling, and our story shall be the education of our heroes.

Courage is knowing what not to fear.

Death is not the worst that can happen to men.

Do not train a child to learn by force or harshness; but direct them to it by what amuses their minds, so that you may be better able to discover with accuracy the peculiar bent of the genius of each.

Education is teaching our children to desire the right things.

Either we shall find what it is we are seeking or at least we shall free ourselves from the persuasion that we know what we do not know.

Every heart sings a song, incomplete, until another heart whispers back. Those who wish to sing always find a song. At the touch of a lover, everyone becomes a poet.

Everything that deceives may be said to enchant.

Evil is the vulgar lover who loves the body rather than the soul, inasmuch as he is not even stable, because he loves a thing which is in itself unstable, and therefore when the bloom of youth which he was desiring is over, he takes wing and flies away, in spite of all his words and promises; whereas the love of the noble disposition is life-long, for it becomes one with the everlasting.

Excellence is not a gift, but a skill that takes practice. We do not act rightly because we are excellent, in fact we achieve excellence by acting rightly.

Excess of liberty, whether it lies in state or individuals, seems only to pass into excess of slavery.

False words are not only evil in themselves, but they infect the soul with evil.

For this feeling of wonder shows that you are a philosopher, since wonder is the only beginning of philosophy.

For to fear death, my friends, is only to think ourselves wise without really being wise, for it is to think that we know what we do not know. For no one knows whether death may not be the greatest good that can happen to man.

Good actions give strength to ourselves and inspire good actions in others.

Good people do not need laws to tell them to act responsibly, while bad people will find a way around the laws.

Have you ever sensed that our soul is immortal and never dies?

He could not harm me, for I do not think it is permitted that a better man be harmed by a worse.

He feels particularly ashamed if ever he is seen by his lovers to be involved in something dishonourable.

He was a wise man who invented God.

He who approaches the temple of the Muses without inspiration, in the belief that craftsmanship alone suffices, will remain a bungler and his presumptuous poetry will be obscured by the songs of the maniacs.

He whom loves touches not walks in darkness.

Honesty is for the most part less profitable than dishonesty.

How can you prove whether at this moment we are sleeping, and all our thoughts are a dream; or whether we are awake, and talking to one another in the waking state?

How could they see anything but the shadows if they were never allowed to move their heads?

Human behavior flows from three main sources: desire, emotion, and knowledge.

I am the wisest man alive, for I know one thing, and that is that I know nothing.

I have hardly ever known a mathematician who was capable of reasoning.

I thought to myself: I am wiser than this man; neither of us probably knows anything that is really good, but he thinks he has knowledge, when he has not, while I, having no knowledge, do not think I have.

I would teach children music, physics, and philosophy; but most importantly music, for the patterns in music and all the arts are the keys to learning.

I'm trying to think, don't confuse me with facts.

Ideas are the source of all things.

If a man can be properly said to love something, it must be clear that he feels affection for it as a whole, and does not love part of it to the exclusion of the rest.

If men learn this, it will implant forgetfulness in their souls; they will cease to exercise memory because they rely on that which is written, calling things to remembrance no longer from within themselves, but by means of external marks. What you have discovered is a recipe not for memory, but for reminder. And it is no true wisdom that you offer your disciples, but only its semblance, for by telling them of many things without teaching them you will make them seem to know much, while for the most part they know nothing, and as men filled, not with wisdom, but with the conceit of wisdom, they will be a burden to their fellows.

If women are expected to do the same work as men, we must teach them the same things.

Ignorance, the root and stem of every evil.

In order for man to succeed in life, God provided him with two means, education and physical activity. Not separately, one for the soul and the other for the body, but for the two together. With these means, man can attain perfection.

In politics we presume that everyone who knows how to get votes knows how to administer a city or a state. When we are ill, we do not ask for the handsomest physician, or the most eloquent one.

In practice people who study philosophy too long become very odd birds, not to say thoroughly vicious; while even those who are the best of them are reduced by philosophy to complete uselessness as members of society.

Is there a perfect world?

It is the task of the enlightened not only to ascend to learning and to see the good but to be willing to descend again to those prisoners and to share their troubles and their honors, whether they are worth having or not. And this they must do, even with the prospect of death.

It's better in fact to be guilty of manslaughter than of fraud about what is fair and just.

Knowledge becomes evil if the aim be not virtuous.

Knowledge is the food of the soul.

Knowledge which is acquired under compulsion has no hold on the mind. Therefore do not use compulsion, but let early education be a sort of amusement; you will then be better able to discover the child's natural bent.

Lack of activity destroys the good condition of every human being.

Let parents then bequeath to their children not riches but the spirit of reverence.

let the speaker speak truly and the judge decide justly.

Love is a serious mental disease.

Love is born into every human being; it calls back the halves of our original nature together; it tries to make one out of two and heal the wound of human nature.

Love is simply the name for the desire and pursuit of the whole.

Love is the pursuit of the whole.

Love' is the name for our pursuit of wholeness, for our desire to be complete.

Man is a being in search of meaning.

Man is a prisoner who has no right to open the door of his prison and run away. A man should wait, and not take his own life until God summons him.

Man is a tame or civilized animal; never the less, he requires proper instruction and a fortunate nature, and then of all animals he becomes the most divine and most civilized; but if he be insufficiently or ill- educated he is the most savage of earthly creatures.

Men of Athens, I honor and love you; but I shall obey God rather than you, and while I have life and strength I shall never cease from the practice and teaching of philosophy. Understand that I shall never alter my ways, not even if I have to die many times.

Money-makers are tiresome company, as they have no standard but cash value.

Musical innovation is full of danger to the State, for when modes of music change, the fundamental laws of the State always change with them.

Musical training is a more potent instrument than any other, because rhythm and harmony find their way into the inward places of the soul.

Necessity is the mother of invention.

*Never discourage anyone who continually makes progress,
no matter how slow.*

No human thing is of serious importance.

*No man should bring children into the world who is unwilling
to persevere to the end in their nature and education.*

No one is more hated than he who speaks the truth.

No wealth can ever make a bad man at peace with himself.

Nothing beautiful without struggle.

Of all the animals, the boy is the most unmanageable.

One of the penalties of refusing to participate in politics is that you end up being governed by your inferiors.

Only a philosopher's mind grows wings, since its memory always keeps it as close as possible to those realities by being close to which the gods are divine.

Only the dead have seen the end of war.

People are like dirt. They can either nourish you and help you grow as a person or they can stunt your growth and make you wilt and die.

Philosophy is the highest music.

Poetry is nearer to vital truth than history.

Poets utter great and wise things which they do not themselves understand.

Strange times are these in which we live when old and young are taught falsehoods in school. And the person that dares to tell the truth is called at once a lunatic and fool.

That's what education should be, I said, the art of orientation. Educators should devise the simplest and most effective methods of turning minds around. It shouldn't be the art of implanting sight in the organ, but should proceed on the understanding that the organ already has the capacity, but is improperly aligned and isn't facing the right way.

The beginning is the most important part of the work.

The difficulty, my friends, is not in avoiding death, but in avoiding unrighteousness; for that runs faster than death.

The direction in which education starts a man will determine his future life.

The first and best victory is to conquer self.

The greatest wealth is to live content with little.

The heaviest penalty for declining to rule is to be ruled by someone inferior to yourself.

The madness of love is the greatest of heaven's blessings.

The man who finds that in the course of his life he has done a lot of wrong often wakes up at night in terror, like a child with a nightmare, and his life is full of foreboding: but the man who is conscious of no wrongdoing is filled with cheerfulness and with the comfort of old age.

The man who makes everything that leads to happiness depends upon himself, and not upon other men, has adopted the very best plan for living happily. This is the man of moderation, the man of manly character and of wisdom.

The measure of a man is what he does with power.

The most effective kind of education is that a child should play amongst lovely things.

The object of education is to teach us to love what is beautiful.

The philosopher whose dealings are with divine order himself acquires the characteristics of order and divinity.

The price good men pay for indifference to public affairs is to be ruled by evil men.

The price of apathy towards public affairs is to be ruled by evil men.

The society we have described can never grow into a reality or see the light of day, and there will be no end to the troubles of states, or indeed, my dear Glaucon, of humanity itself, till philosophers become rulers in this world, or till those we now call kings and rulers really and truly become philosophers, and political power and philosophy thus come into the same hands.

The soul of man is immortal and imperishable.

The soul takes flight to the world that is invisible but there arriving she is sure of bliss and forever dwells in paradise.

The soul takes nothing with her to the next world but her education and her culture. At the beginning of the journey to the next world, one's education and culture can either provide the greatest assistance, or else act as the greatest burden, to the person who has just died.

The unexamined life is not worth living.

There are three classes of men; lovers of wisdom, lovers of honor, and lovers of gain.

There are two things a person should never be angry at, what they can help, and what they cannot.

There is also a third kind of madness, which is possession by the Muses, enters into a delicate and virgin soul, and there inspiring frenzy, awakens lyric. But he, who, not being inspired and having no touch of madness in his soul, comes to the door and thinks he will get into the temple by the help of art--he, I say, and his poetry are not admitted; the sane man is nowhere at all when he enters into rivalry with the madman.

There is in every one of us, even those who seem to be most moderate, a type of desire that is terrible, wild, and lawless.

There is truth in wine and children.

This and no other is the root from which a tyrant springs; when he first appears he is a protector.

Those who are able to see beyond the shadows and lies of their culture will never be understood, let alone believed, by the masses.

Those who are too smart to engage in politics are punished by being governed by those who are dumber.

Those who don't know must learn from those who do.

Those who tell the stories rule society.

Time is the moving image of reality.

To be afraid of death is only another form of thinking that one is wise when one is not; it is to think that one knows what one does not know. No one knows with regard to death whether it is not really the greatest blessing that can happen to man; but people dread it as though they were certain it is the greatest evil.

To conquer oneself is the best and noblest victory; to be vanquished by one's own nature is the worst and most ignoble defeat.

True friendship can exist only between equals.

We are like people looking for something they have in their hands all the time; we're looking in all directions except at the thing we want, which is probably why we haven't found it.

We can easily forgive a child who is afraid of the dark; the real tragedy of life is when men are afraid of the light.

We do not learn, and that what we call learning is only a process of recollection.

What if the man could see Beauty Itself, pure, unalloyed, stripped of mortality, and all its pollution, stains, and vanities, unchanging, divine, the man becoming in that communion, the friend of God, himself immortal; would that be a life to disregard?

When he looks at Beauty in the only way that Beauty can be seen - only then will it become possible for him to give birth not to images of virtue (because he's in touch with no images), but to true virtue (because he is in touch with true Beauty). The love of the gods belongs to anyone who has given to true virtue and nourished it, and if any human being could become immortal, it would be he.

When men speak ill of thee, live so as nobody may believe them.

When one of them meets the other half, the actual half of himself, whether he be a lover of youth or a lover of another sort, the pair are lost in an amazement of love and friendship and intimacy and one will not be out of the other's sight, as I may say, even for a moment.

When someone sees a soul disturbed and unable to see something, he won't laugh mindlessly, but he'll take into consideration whether it has come from a brighter life and is dimmed through not having yet become accustomed to the dark or whether it has come from greater ignorance into greater light and is dazzled by the increased brilliance.

When the tyrant has disposed of foreign enemies by conquest or treaty and there is nothing to fear from them then he is always stirring up some wary or other in order that the people may require a leader.

When there is an income tax, the just man will pay more and the unjust less on the same amount of income.

Wise men speak because they have something to say; fools because they have to say something.

Wise men talk because they have something to say; Fools, because they have to say something.

Writing is the geometry of the soul.

You know that the beginning is the most important part of any work, especially in the case of a young and tender thing; for that is the time at which the character is being formed and the desired impression is more readily taken. Shall we just carelessly allow children to hear any casual tales which may be devised by casual persons, and to receive into their minds ideas for the most part the very opposite of those which we should wish them to have when they are grown up?

We cannot. Anything received into the mind at that age is likely to become indelible and unalterable; and therefore it is most important that the tales which the young first hear should be models of virtuous thoughts.

You should not honor men more than truth.

You're my Star, a stargazer too, and I wish that I were Heaven, with a billion eyes to look at you!

www.ingramcontent.com/pod-product-compliance
Lightning Source LLC
Chambersburg PA
CBHW071256070526
44583CB00017B/2492